Calligraphy Meets Philosophy

Talk 2

尚語

第二話

KS Vincent POON（潘君尚）

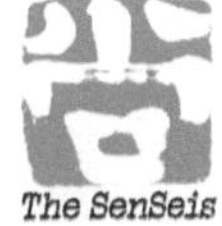

First Edition
Aug 2023

Published by
The SenSeis 尚尚齋
Toronto
Canada
www.thesenseis.com
publishing@thesenseis.com

ISBN 978-1-989485-32-3

Cover
Tochoji Temple
東長寺
Fukuoka Japan

In Loving Memory of My Beloved Mother

Pui Luen Nora TSANG（曾佩鑾）

Table of Contents

Longya Judun, A Zen Poem Ⅱ（龍牙居遁 禪詩之二）

Longya Judun, A Zen Poem Ⅲ（龍牙居遁 禪詩之三）

"Withstand and Endure", with Kuiji's Annotation（"堪忍", 窺基贊文）

Diamond Sutra in Small Standard Script（小楷 《 金剛般若波羅蜜經 》）

Calligraphy Meets Philosophy - Talk 2

Introduction

(I)

Content is the soul of an artwork.

Thus, catching the soul of Chinese calligraphy requires understanding the literary contents. To facilitate this, the *Calligraphy Meets Philosophy* series presents traditional Chinese calligraphy alongside line-by-line translated texts with remarks and footnotes. As such, it furthers readers' understanding of traditional Chinese thoughts through calligraphy and concise English translations.

(II)

Calligraphy Meets Philosophy – Talk 2 (《尚語•第二話》) highlights some key traditional Chinese philosophical concepts like "Nothingness (空)", "Form (色)", "Tranquility (靜)", "Ease (閒)", and "Self Enlightenment (自我覺悟)". It does so by having calligraphies and translations of selected literary works by Cao Cao (曹操, 155-220 AD), Zhuge Liang (諸葛亮, 181-234 AD), Yen Shang (楊慎, 1488–1559 AD), Bai Juyi (白居易, 772-846 AD), Li Bai (李白, 701-762 AD), The Nun of the Wujinzhan (無盡藏比丘尼, ?-?AD), Wuzu Fayan (五祖法演, ?-1104AD), Longya Judun (龍牙居遁, 835-923 AD), and Kuiji (窺基, 632-682 AD). The concluding artwork is my calligraphy of the entire *Diamond Sutra* (《金剛般若波羅蜜經》) in small standard script (小楷), followed by a short remark.

(III)

This book could not have been published without the help of my father, Dr Kwok Kin POON (潘國鍵博士). I sincerely thank his priceless advice on my translations throughout the series. His unwavering support and tutelage have always been the chief drivers of my passion for learning and passing on traditional Chinese calligraphy and culture.

Knowledge is never pursued alone.

KS Vincent Poon
August 2023, Toronto

Cao Cao
Behold the Turquoise Sea

曹操
《觀滄海》

Calligraphy

Calligrapher (書者): KS Vincent Poon (潘君尚)

Content (內容): *Behold the Turquoise Sea,* a poem by Cao Cao (曹操《觀滄海》)

Style (字體): Standard Script (楷書)

Caption (款識): 曹操步出夏門行之觀滄海壬寅潘君尚書於尚齋 (Cao Cao *Marched Out the Grand Illustrious Gate's Behold the Turquoise Sea,* year of the Renyin, Kwan Sheung Vincent Poon scribed at The Senseis)

Seal Inscription (鈐印): 君尚 (朱文) (Kwan Sheung Vincent, red characters), 潘 (白文) (Poon, white character)

Medium (材料): Ink on Xuan paper (紙墨水本)

Size (尺寸): 112 X 50cm

Year (年份): 2022

東臨碣石，以觀滄海。水何澹澹，山島竦峙。樹木叢生，百草豐茂。秋風蕭瑟，洪波湧起。日月之行，若出其中。星漢燦爛，若出其裏。幸甚至哉，歌以詠志。

曹操步出夏門行之觀滄海　壬寅潘君尚書於尚尚齋

Translation

曹操《觀滄海》
Cao Cao, *Behold the Turquoise Sea*

1. 東臨碣石，
I approached the east and climbed Jieshi mountain (碣石)[1],

2. 以觀滄海。
So I could behold the turquoise sea.

3. 水何澹澹，
Waters, how wavy (澹澹) indeed,

4. 山島竦峙。
Islands stood tall amidst the waves.

5. 樹木叢生，
Trees were abundant,

6. 百草豐茂。
Turfs were luxuriant.

7. 秋風蕭瑟，
Autumn winds blew cold and bleak,

8. 洪波湧起。
Gigantic billows ascended from the sea.

9. 日月之行，
As the Sun and Moon rose and set,

10. 若出其中;
They appeared to emerge from it;

11. 星漢粲爛 ,
Even the bright and brilliant stars in the sky,

12. 若出其裏。
All seemed to be delivered by it.

13. 幸甚至哉！
Truly blessed to be here, indeed![2]

14. 歌以詠志。
By chanting this, I proclaim my aspirations.[3]

(translated by KS Vincent Poon, Oct. 2015; revised Oct. 2022)

Remarks

(I)

Behold the Turquoise Sea (《觀滄海》) belongs to *Marched Out the Grand Illustrious Gate* (《步出夏門行》), written by Cao Cao (曹操, 155-220 AD)[4]. It was phrased in a folk-song style of the Yuefu (樂府, "The Imperial Music Bureau") format, which was prevalent during the Han Dynasty [5].

Cao Cao is one of the most influential warlords of the Three Dynasty Period (三國時代, 184-280 AD)[6]. He and his two sons, Cao Pi (曹丕) and Cao Zhi (曹植), are also regarded as outstanding literati[7,8].

(II)

Behold the Turquoise Sea was composed in 207 AD when Cao Cao had conquered the Northeastern parts of China[9]. This poem reflected his great pride and joy as he aspired to unify China under his rule [10]. Yet, a year after writing this poem, his conceitedness led him to suffer great losses in the Battle of Red Cliffs (赤壁之戰, 208 AD). All vanquished into "nothingness (空)", and his plans to unify China never succeeded.

 "There is no greater tragedy than underestimating or disregarding one's enemy (禍莫大於輕敵)", Laozi (老子) of the 6th Century BC once wrote[11]. Cao's defeat at the Red Cliffs proved Laozi was right once again.

Footnotes

(1). "碣石, 山名, 原在今河北樂亭縣西南, 後世沉陷到海裏." See 王力 《古代漢語》. Beijing: 中華書局, 1998 edition, p.1393.

(2). Some contend "幸甚至哉" was placed for rhythmical purposes and not related to the textual content ("配合樂曲時所加的，和正文無關"). See 王力, ibid., p.1393.

However,"幸甚至哉" may be relevant, for it could express Cao Cao's emotions in reaching the Jieshi, as narrated in the poem's preamble:

經過至我碣石，心惆悵我東海。
Source: 余冠英 《三曹詩選 》. Beijing：人民文學出版社, 1961, p.6.

Therefore, it is not unreasonable to interpret "幸甚至哉" as "Truly blessed to be here, indeed".

(3). Some contend "歌以詠志", like "幸甚至哉", was also placed for rhythmical purposes and not related to the textual content. See 王力, ibid, p.1393.

However, according to the *Book of Documents* (《尚書》) :

> 詩言志，歌永言。
> Poems were composed to express one's mind and aspirations, while songs were chanted to express one's narratives.
> (translated by KS Vincent Poon)
> Source: 孔安國《尚書孔傳•虞書•舜典》.Taipei: 新興書局, 1964, p.008.

Therefore, "歌以詠志" was not completely meaningless.

(4). 余冠英, 《三曹詩選》. Beijing：人民文學出版社, 1961, p.6.

(5). 鄭振鐸, 《中國文學史》. Shanghai: 商務印書館, 1932, p.131.

(6). 陳壽, 《三國志》, 魏志 Vol. 1, 武帝操. Taipei: 中華書局, 1968, pp.1-3.

(7). 王力, as in footnote (1), pp.1392-1394, and p.1397.

(8). 鄭振鐸 , as in footnote (5), pp.131-140.

(9). 王力, as in footnote (1), p.1393.

(10). 鄭振鐸, as in footnote (5), p.132.

(11). KS Vincent Poon & Kwok Kin Poon, *An English Translation and the Correct Interpretation of Laozi's Tao Te Ching*. Toronto: The SenSeis, 2020, p.65.

16

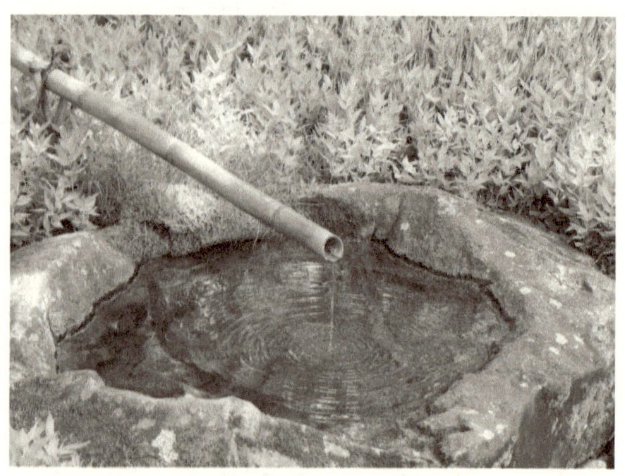

A Tranquil Fountain in MOA Museum of Art
MOA美術館恬静小泉水
Atami Japan
Photographed by KS Vincent Poon
2023

Zhuge Liang
"Tranquillity Allows One to Arrive at Thinking Deeply and Extensively"

諸葛亮
"寧靜致遠"

寧靜致遠

Calligraphy

Calligrapher (書者): KS Vincent Poon (潘君尚)

Content (內容): Tranquillity Allows One to Arrive at Thinking Deeply and Extensively (寧靜致遠)

Style (字體): Clerical Script (隸書)

Caption (款識): 君尚 (Kwan Sheung Vincent)

Seal Inscription (鈐印): 潘氏 (白文) (The Surname of Poon, white characters)

Medium (材料): Ink on Xuan paper (紙墨水本)

Size (尺寸): 16 X 27 cm

Year (年份): 2016

Translation

"寧靜致遠"
"Tranquillity allows one to arrive at thinking deeply and extensively"

Remarks

(I)

"Tranquillity allows one to arrive at thinking deeply and extensively (寧靜致遠)" is a paraphrase of a passage in Zhuge Liang's (諸葛亮, 181-234 AD) *Admonition to His Son* (誡子書)[1]:

> 夫君子之行，靜以修身，儉以養德。非澹泊無以明志，**非寧靜無以致遠。**
>
> Alas, this is the path that an honourable person should take: apply tranquillity to cultivate the self, pursue frugality to raise one's morality. Without leaving behind materialistic ambitions, one cannot see (明) one's true aspiration; **without tranquillity, one cannot arrive at (致) thinking deeply and extensively (遠).**[2]
>
> (translated by KS Vincent Poon, Aug. 2016; revised Oct. 2022)

(II)

Zhuge Liang is a symbol of wisdom and integrity in East Asian societies. He served as the prime minister and chief military strategist for the Shu Han Kingdom (蜀漢) during the Three Kingdoms Period of China (三國時代, 184-280). Liu Bei (劉備), the ruler of Shu Han, had to visit him three times before he agreed to help him[3].

(III)

The importance of filling the mind with tranquillity can be traced to Laozi (老子) of the 6th century BC. In the canonical Taoist text *Tao Te Ching* (《道德經》), he proclaimed "one should always hold simplicity and tranquillity in highest regard (恬淡為上)"[4] and "pristine tranquillity is the true guiding principle of all under Heaven (清靜為天下正)"[5].

Footnotes

(1). 《太平御覽》Vol. 459, 人事部一百 "鑒戒下". 京都東福寺東京靜嘉堂文庫藏宋刊本, p8a.

(2). "非寧靜無以致遠" is often generally interpreted as "tranquillity is required to reach one's far-reaching goals (心境安寧清靜，才能達到遠大目標)".

Yet, judging from the source and usage of this sentence, this sort of interpretation is very doubtful. In *Huainanzi - Craft of the Ruler* (《淮南子•主術訓》) :

是故非澹薄無以明德，非寧靜無以致遠，非寬大無以兼覆，非慈厚無以懷眾，非平正無以制斷。
Source: 劉文典《淮南鴻烈集解》, Book 3, Vol 9, 主術訓. Shanghai: 商務印書館, 1933, p.16.

"明德", "并覆", "制斷", "兼覆", "懷眾" all describe states of mind (心境). "致遠" thus refers to the mind, not any far-reaching physical goals. "遠 (far and deep)" should therefore be better taken as "thinking deeply and extensively".

The contention of tranquillity resulting in a far and deep mind is not uncommon in Chinese thoughts. An excellent example can be seen in the Confucian canon, *Great Learning* (《大學》):

靜而后能安，安而后能慮，慮而后能得。
With unmoved tranquillity, one then can be at ease (安) under any circumstance. With being at ease under any circumstance, one then can deliberate (慮) with great care. With deliberating with great care, one then can attain (得) the highest excellence.
Source: KS Vincent Poon *Calligraphy Meets Philosophy - Talk 1*. Toronto: The SenSeis, 2022, p.24.

(3). 陳壽,《三國志》, 蜀志 Vol. 5, 諸葛亮. Taipei: 中華書局, 1968, p.2.

(4). KS Vincent Poon & Kwok Kin Poon, *An English Translation and the Correct Interpretation of Laozi's Tao Te Ching*. Toronto: The SenSeis, 2020, p.37.

(5). Ibid., p.47.

Yang Shen
The Immortals by the River

楊慎
《臨江仙》

Calligraphy

Calligrapher (書者): KS Vincent Poon (潘君尚)

Content (內容): *The Immortals by the River,* a poem by Yang Shen (楊慎《臨江仙》)

Style (字體): Standard, Semi-cursive, and Cursive Scripts (楷書, 行書, 草書)

Caption (款識): 楊慎臨江仙二千十六年仲夏潘君尚書於尚尚齋 (Yang Shen *The Immortals by the River,* mid summer in the year of two-thousand and sixteen, Kwan Sheung Vincent Poon scribed at The Senseis)

Seal Inscription (鈐印): 君尚 (朱文) (Kwan Sheung Vincent, red characters), 潘 (白文) (Poon, white character)

Medium (材料): Ink on Xuan paper (紙墨水本)

Size (尺寸): 120 X 47cm

Year (年份): 2016

滚滚长江东逝水，浪花淘尽英雄。是非成败转头空。青山依旧在，几度夕阳红。

白发渔樵江渚上，惯看秋月春风。一壶浊酒喜相逢。古今多少事，都付笑谈中。

杨慎临江仙 二千十六年仲夏 沐灵尚士书于当二都

Translation

楊慎《臨江仙》
Yang Shen, *The Immortals by the River*

1. 滾滾長江東逝水，浪花淘盡英雄。
The gushing Yangzi waters disappear into the East, their billows washing away all heroes of mighty feats.

2. 是非成敗轉頭空。
Whatever right, wrong, triumph, or failure all instantly turned into nothingness with great speed.

3. 青山依舊在，幾度夕陽紅。
Yet, the green hills still exist, the sun sets in red and repeats.

4. 白髮漁樵江渚上，慣看秋月春風。
An old fisherman and an elderly wood logger are on a patch upon a river, both accustomed to appreciating the autumn moons and the spring breeze.

5. 一壺濁酒喜相逢。
A bottle of crude wine is shared as the two joyously meet.

6. 古今多少事，都付笑談中!
Countless affairs of the past and present shall be relegated to amusing gossips indeed!

(translated by KS Vincent Poon, Oct. 2015; revised Dec. 2022)

Remarks

(I)

Ming Dynasty's Yang Shen (楊慎, 1488–1559 AD) wrote this poem as the lyrics to the song *The Immortals by the River* (《臨江仙》)[1]. This poem became extremely popular ever since Mao Zonggang (毛宗崗, 1632-1709) applied it as an overture to Luo Guanzhong's (羅貫中, 1330 - 1400) acclaimed novel *Romance of the Three Kingdoms* (《三國演義》)[2].

(II)

The calligraphy presented here is a mixture of standard, semi-cursive, and cursive script characters. This rather unorthodox approach can also be seen in Yan Zhenqing's (顏真卿) masterpiece *A Poem on General Pei* (《裴將軍詩》)[3].

In the calligraphy, the "二" below "滾" means "a character as above", for "二" is "上 (above)" in seal script (篆書).

(III)

It is important to note "nothingness (空)" here does not mean "non-existence". It should be better interpreted as "non-concrete existence (非實有)", for all human affairs are fleeting and cannot be considered eternal entities. Thus, one should always let go. This is akin to the "nothingness (空)" in the Buddhist canon *Heart Sutra* (《般若波羅蜜多心經》)[4].

Footnotes

(1). 楊慎，《廿一史彈詞註・第三段・說秦漢》. Guangzhou: 中華書局, 1939, p.69.

(2). 李萬鈞，《中西文學類型比較史》. Taipei: 萬卷樓圖書公司, 2018, p.291.

(3). KS Vincent Poon & Kwok Kin Poon, *English Translation of Classical Chinese Calligraphy Masterpieces*. Toronto: The Sen-Seis, 2019, pp.81-92.

(4). KS Vincent Poon, *Calligraphy Meets Philosophy - Talk 1*. Toronto: The SenSeis, 2022, pp.10-15.

Bai Juyi
The Restricted Central Area of the Imperial Palace

白居易
《禁中》

Calligraphy

Calligrapher (書者): KS Vincent Poon (潘君尚)

Content (內容): *The Restricted Central Area of the Imperial Palace,* a poem by Bai Juyi (白居易《禁中》)

Style (字體): Cursive Script (草書)

Caption (款識): 白居易禁中壬寅君尚 (Bai Juyi *The Restricted Central Area of the Imperial Palace*, year of the Renyin, Kwan Sheung Vincent)

Seal Inscription (鈐印): 君尚 (朱文) (Kwan Sheung Vincent, red characters), 潘氏 (白文) (The Surname of Poon, white characters)

Medium (材料): Ink on Xuan paper (紙墨水本)

Size (尺寸): 64 X 32cm

Year (年份): 2022

了龍如重郭窗遠一

宅眉好光陰心雲何

幽居在深山

白居易句　葉中壬亥書

Translation

白居易《禁中》
Bai Juyi, *The Restricted Central Area of the Imperial Palace*

1. 門嚴九重靜,
The solemn doors and its majestic palace are all quiet with much peace,

2. 窗幽一室閑。
The tranquil windows and its solitary room are full of ample ease.

3. 好是修心處,
Such is truly (好是)[1] the place to cultivate one's mind,

4. 何必在深山?
Why must it be done deep in the mountains all the time?

(translated by KS Vincent Poon, May 2022)

Remarks

(I)

This poem was composed by the renowned Tang Dynasty poet Bai Juyi (白居易,772-846 AD)[2]. It was authored around 808-810AD when Bai was appointed as a junior officer to identify any imperial oversight (左拾遺)[3]. At roughly the same time, he was also bestowed by the Emperor the title of "Scholar of the Hanlin

Academy (翰林學士)"[4].

(II)

Under these favourable circumstances, Bai was probably full of himself and blind to the substantial power struggles and mundane matters in the imperial bureaucracy. Indeed, the doors and windows in the palace might be all quiet, but the minds in there were never at complete ease. How can that be compared to a truly isolated place deep in the mountains?

Footnotes

(1). "好是" means "正是 (is truly)", as in Yuan Jie's (元結) *Ai Nai Qu* (《欸乃曲》): "停橈靜聽曲中意，好是雲山韶濩音." See《全唐詩》compiled by 曹寅, Vol. 241. 欽定四庫全書薈要集部全唐詩, 康熙四十六年版, p.22.

(2). 《全唐詩》Vol.428 , ibid., p.7.

(3). 朱金城,《白居易集箋校》. Shanghai: 上海古籍出版社, 1988, pp.3 & 285.

(4). Ibid., p.3.

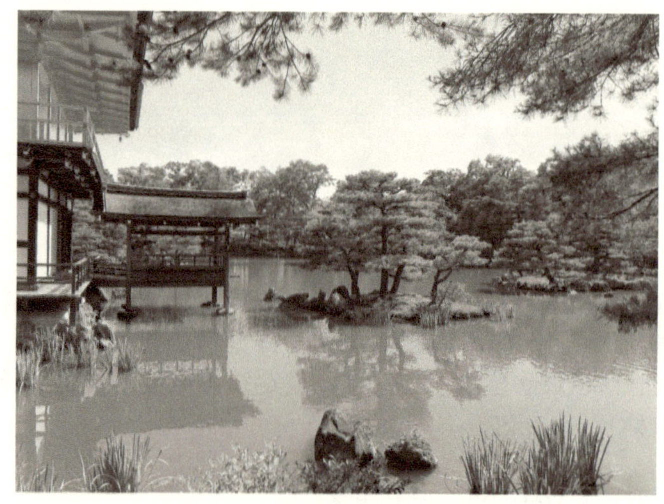

Kinkaku-ji Temple Ginga Spring

金閣寺銀河泉

Kyoto Japan

Photographed by KS Vincent Poon

2012

Bai Juyi
The Baiyun Spring

白居易
《白雲泉》

Calligraphy

Calligrapher (書者): KS Vincent Poon (潘君尚)

Content (內容): *The Baiyun Spring,* a poem by Bai Juyi (白居易《白雲泉》)

Style (字體): Clerical Script (隸書)

Caption (款識): 白居易白雲泉詩意即老子所言守靜篤癸卯潘君尚 (The gist of Bai Juyi *The Baiyun Spring* is Laozi's safeguard tranquilities with absolute diligence. Year of the Guimao, Kwan Sheung Vincent Poon)

Seal Inscription (鈐印): 君尚 (朱文) (Kwan Sheung Vincent, red characters), 潘氏 (白文) (The Surname of Poon, white characters)

Medium (材料): Ink on Xuan paper (紙墨水本)

Size (尺寸): 64 X 35cm

Year (年份): 2023

天平山上白雲泉，雲自無心水自閑。
何必奔衝下山去，更添波浪在人間。

白居易白雲泉詩一首 老子曰六十有一 翁選 癸卯 沈定盦

Translation

白居易《白雲泉》
Bai Juyi, *The Baiyun Spring*

1. 天平山上白雲泉，
Upon the Tianping Mountain lies the Baiyun Spring,

2. 雲自無心水自閒。
Where clouds are naturally carefree, and waters are naturally resting.

3. 何必奔衝下山去，
Why then should the waters rush down the mountain rapidly,

4. 更添波浪在人間？
To cause even more turbulent billows amongst humanity?

(translated by KS Vincent Poon, June 2022)

Remarks

(I)

This poem was composed by the renowned poet Bai Juyi (白居易,772-846 AD) in 825AD when he was relegated to being the Governor of Suzhou (蘇州刺史) [1,2]. This was about ten years after he was demoted and exiled from the capital in 815AD[3].

(II)

Unlike his previous work, *The Restricted Central Area of the Imperial Palace* (《禁中》), Bai probably realized he was never at peace while working in a bureaucracy, especially inside the imperial palace. Through experiencing dirty power struggles, Bai matured and finally understood the essential difference between a treacherous palace and a secluded place deep in the mountains.

To end up living in seclusion is generally the fate of a traditional Chinese intellect. Bai was no exception.

Footnotes

(1). 《全唐詩》 compiled by 曹寅, Vol. 462. 欽定四庫全書薈要集部全唐詩, 康熙四十六年版, p.11.

(2). 上海辭書出版社, 《唐詩鑒賞辭典》. Shanghai: 上海辭書出版社, 2004, p.921.

(3). 朱金城,《白居易集箋校》. Shanghai: 上海古籍出版社, 1988, p.3.

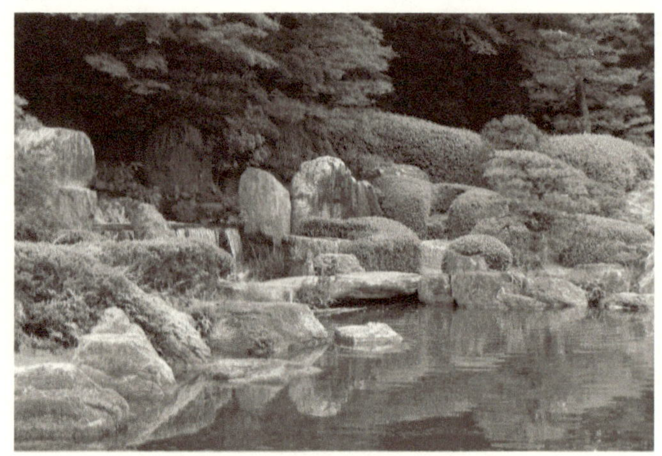

Ohori Park Japanese Garden
大濠公園日本庭園
Fukuoka Japan
Photographed by KS Vincent Poon
2023

Li Bai
Replying to a Query at the Hills

李白
《山中問答》

Calligraphy

Calligrapher (書者): KS Vincent Poon (潘君尚)

Content (內容): *Replying to a Query at the Hills,* a poem by Li Bai (李白《山中問答》)

Style (字體): Standard Script (楷書)

Caption (款識): 全唐詩李白山中問答壬寅潘君尚於尚尚齋 (*The Complete Tang Poems,* Li Bai, *Replying to a Query at the Hills.* Year of the Renyin, Kwan Sheung Vincent Poon at The Senseis)

Seal Inscription (鈐印): 君尚 (朱文) (Kwan Sheung Vincent, red characters), 潘氏 (白文) (The Surname of Poon, white characters)

Medium (材料): Ink on Xuan paper (紙墨水本)

Size (尺寸): 64 X 35cm

Year (年份): 2022

問余何意栖碧山笑而不答心自閒桃花流水窅然去別有天地非人間

全唐詩李白山中問答　壬寅潘君尚於尚尚齋

Translation

李白《山中問答》
Li Bai, *Replying to a Query at the Hills*

1. 問余何意栖碧山，
I was once asked why I longed (意)[1] to reside in seclusion (栖)[2] deep in the green hills,

2. 笑而不答心自閒。
Smiling and offering no reply, my mind was at ease and self-fulfilled (自閒)[3].

3. 桃花流水窅然去，
In the forest of peach blossoms, along the flowing stream, I went towards the very deep and serene (窅然)[4] place upon the hills,

4. 別有天地非人間。
Alas, another new world not of the human realm was revealed.

(translated by KS Vincent Poon, July 2022)

Remarks

(I)

This poem was composed by the eminent poet Li Bai (李白, 701-762 AD) between 729 to 730AD[5]. At that time, Li was living in seclusion at An Lui (安陸).

(II)

To correctly interpret this poem, one must first understand it was written in reference to Tao Yuanming's (陶淵明, 365-427 AD) masterpiece, *Peach Blossom Spring* (《 桃花源記 》). In it, a fisherman discovered a secluded Utopia upon a hill by going **against** a river stream amidst a forest of peach trees[6]. In Lines 3 and 4 of this poem, Li likened himself to that particular fisherman who longed to live in a perfectly secluded Utopia.

Thus, interpreting "桃花流水窅然去" as something like "the peach blossoms, carried by the stream, flows deeply and tranquilly away"[7] is not correct. If the peach blossoms were flowing with the stream, they would have travelled down the hill and never reached the "new world" in Line 4. The correct vernacular Chinese interpretation of Line 3 should be:

在桃花林沿著溪流，往山上幽深處去。
(by Kwok Kin Poon, July 2022)

Footnotes

(1). "意" here means "desire/long for (心所嚮也) ", as indicated in《增修互注禮部韻略》compiled by 毛晃, Vol.4. See 欽定四庫全書經部十, 小學類, 康熙四十四年版, p.21.

(2). "栖" here means "live in seclusion (栖遲/隱居)", as in 潘岳
《許由頌》："澹泊無營，栖遲高山." See 嚴可均 《全晉文》 Vol.
92. Beijing: 商務印書館, 1999, p.984.　Further, in《全唐詩》,
the character is "栖" not "樓".　See《全唐詩》 compiled by 曹寅,
Vol.178. 欽定四庫全書薈要集部全唐詩, 康熙四十六年版, p. 2.

(3). "自聞" here means "at ease and self-fulfilled (悠閒自得)". See
《漢語大詞典》Vol.8 . Shanghai: 上海辭書出版社, 2008, p.1330.

(4). "窅然" here means "deep and serene (深遠幽暗的樣子)". See
《漢語大詞典》Vol.8 . Shanghai: 上海辭書出版社, 2008, p.438.

(5). 《李白選集》annotated by 郁賢皓. Shanghai: 上海古籍出版
社, 2012, p.33.

(6). In *Peach Blossom Springs* （《桃花源記》):

    晉太元中, 武陵人, 捕魚為業. 緣溪行, 忘路之遠近. 忽逢桃花林 …
In the reign of Taiyuan of Jin Dynasty, there was a man of Wuling
who was a fisherman by trade. One day he was fishing **up** a stream
in his boat, heedless of how far he had gone, when suddenly he
came upon a forest of peach trees...
Source: Xianyi Yang (楊憲益) *Poetry and Prose of the Han, Wei and
Six Dynasties.* Beijing: Panda Books, 1986, p.63.

(7). 俞平伯《唐詩鑒賞辭典》:"詩雖寫花隨溪水, 窅然遠逝的景色,
..." Shanghai: 上海辭書出版社, 2004, p.321.

The Nun of the Wujinzhan
An Ode to Plum Blossoms

無盡藏比丘尼
《詠梅花》

Calligraphy

Calligrapher (書者): KS Vincent Poon (潘君尚)

Content (內容): *An Ode to Plum Blossoms* by The Nun of the Wujinzhan (無盡藏比丘尼《詠梅花》)

Style (字體): Standard Script (楷書)

Caption (款識): 此禪宗佛性不勞外求之理壬寅冬月潘君尚書古禪詩 (Such is the Zen-Buddhist principle that one's inherent Buddha does not need to be sought externally. A winter month during the year of the Renyin, Kwan Sheung Vincent Poon scribed an age-old Zen poem)

Seal Inscription (鈐印): 君尚 (朱文) (Kwan Sheung Vincent, red characters), 潘氏 (白文) (The Surname of Poon, white characters)

Medium (材料): Ink on Xuan paper (紙墨水本)

Size (尺寸): 60 X 30cm

Year (年份): 2022

終日尋春不見春，芒鞋踏破嶺頭雲。歸來偶把梅花嗅，春在枝頭已十分。

此禪宗佛性不勞外求之理　壬寅冬月潘君尚書古禪詩

Translation

無盡藏比丘尼 《詠梅花》
The Nun of the Wujinzhan, *An Ode to Plum Blossoms*

1. 終日尋春不見春，
All day, I journeyed to appreciate the colours of spring (尋春)[1],
yet I see no such thing,

2. 芒鞋踏破嶺頭雲。
My straw shoes were tattered from my steps on the peaks, with
clouds as a surrounding.

3. 歸來偶把梅花嗅，
Upon return, I nonchalantly took a plum blossom and caught a
whiff,

4. 春在枝頭已十分。
The full colours of spring were already on its very tip.

(translated by KS Vincent Poon, February 2022)

Remarks

(I)

This classical Zen-Buddhist (禪宗) poem was rumoured to be

composed by "The Nun of the Wujinzhan" (無盡藏比丘尼) of the Tang Dynasty (618-907AD)[2]. A similar version of this poem is documented in *Yuan Shih Chi Shih* (《元詩紀事》), which attributed the work to a person named "The Nun of the Plum Blossoms (梅花尼)"[3].

(II)

For Zen-Buddhists, True Wisdom (般若智) is intrinsic, not from any external means (一切般若智，皆從自性而生，不從外入)[4]. As such, enlightenment can be achieved in an instant by a spontaneously thought in the mind (一念悟時，眾生是佛)[5]. Enlightenment, like the colours of spring in this poem, is thus nearby, and so no onerous labour is required to find it.

Footnotes

(1). "尋春" here is not "looking for Spring" nor "searching for Spring". "尋春" means "appreciating the colours of spring (遊賞春景)":

    i. 陳子昂 《晦日宴高氏林亭》詩：" 尋春遊上路，追宴入山家."
    ii. 惠洪 《意行入古寺》詩：" 清明雨過快晴天，古寺尋春亦偶然."
    iii. 梁辰魚《浣紗記•遊春》：" 下官就是越國上大夫范蠡，尋春到此."
    iv. 徐元正 《廣陵懷古》詩：" 尋春易過佳風月，送老難忘好墓田."
    Source: 《漢語大詞典》Vol. 2. Shanghai: 上海辭書出版社, 2008, p.1290.

(2). 星雲大師，《千江映月—星雲說偈 1》. Taipei: 佛光文化, 2001, p.18.

(3). The relevant entry in *Yuan Shih Chi Shih* （《元詩紀事》）
depicts the following:

梅花尼 《詠梅花》：" 終日尋春不見春, 芒鞵踏破嶺頭雲. 歸來笑捻梅花
嗅, 春在枝頭已十分."
Source: 陳衍《元詩紀事》Vol. 38. Shanghai: 商務印書館, 1936,
p.687.

(4). 《六祖壇經白話句解》. Hong Kong: 菩提學社, publication
year unknown, p.57.

(5). Ibid., p.69.

Wuzu Fayan
A Zen Poem

五祖法演
禪詩一首

Calligraphy

Calligrapher (書者): KS Vincent Poon (潘君尚)

Content (內容): A Zen poem by Wuzu Fayan (五祖法演禪詩一首)

Style (字體): Clerical Script (隸書)

Caption (款識): 北宋法演詩偈二千二十三年歲次癸卯潘君尚書 (A hymnal poem by Fayan of the Northern Song dynasty. The year two-thousand twenty-three, the year of the Gui-mao, scribed by Kwan Sheung Vincent Poon)

Seal Inscription (鈐印): 君尚 (朱文) (Kwan Sheung Vincent, red characters), 潘氏 (白文) (The Surname of Poon, white characters)

Medium (材料): Ink on Xuan paper (紙墨水本)

Size (尺寸): 68 X 35cm

Year (年份): 2023

洞裏無雲別有天　桃華似
錦柳如煙仙家不解論冬
夏石爛松枯不記年

如京沈琼詩偈二十三年來以癸卯沈君尚書

Translation

五祖法演 禪詩一首
A Zen poem by Wuzu Fayan

1. 洞裏無雲別有天,
It is all clear without any cloud in the transcendental cave, yet another world exists within,

2. 桃花似錦柳如煙。
Peach blossoms are like glamourous silks, while willows are akin to mists of emerald green.

3. 仙家不解論冬夏,
The transcended ones do not understand why commoners talk about winters and summers,

4. 石爛松枯不記年。
For even when the rocks crumble and the pines wither, none remembers the years.

(translated by KS Vincent Poon, February 2022)

Remarks

(I)

This poem is composed by Northern Song Dynasty's Wuzu Fayan

(五祖法演, ?-1104AD)[1], who is often regarded as one of the most influential Zen Buddhist monks in his times[2].

(II)

The poem's first part suggests Zen Buddhists are clear of any mundane thoughts and rest in a realm full of inherent natural beauty. The second part elaborates that the enlightened have already let go of all human concepts like seasons and years. Such is an illustration of a key principle in the canonical *Diamond Sutra* (《金剛經》): "Freed from all perceived ideas, they are thus called Buddha (離一切諸相，即名諸佛)."[3]

Footnotes

(1). 《法演禪師語錄》edited by 才良, Vol.1. Taipei: Chinese Buddhist Electronic Text Association (中華電子佛典協會, CBETA).

(2). 《五燈會元》by 普濟, Vol.19. Ibid..

(3). 《金剛經白話句解》. Hong Kong: 菩提學社, publication year unknown, p.62. Translated by KS Vincent Poon.

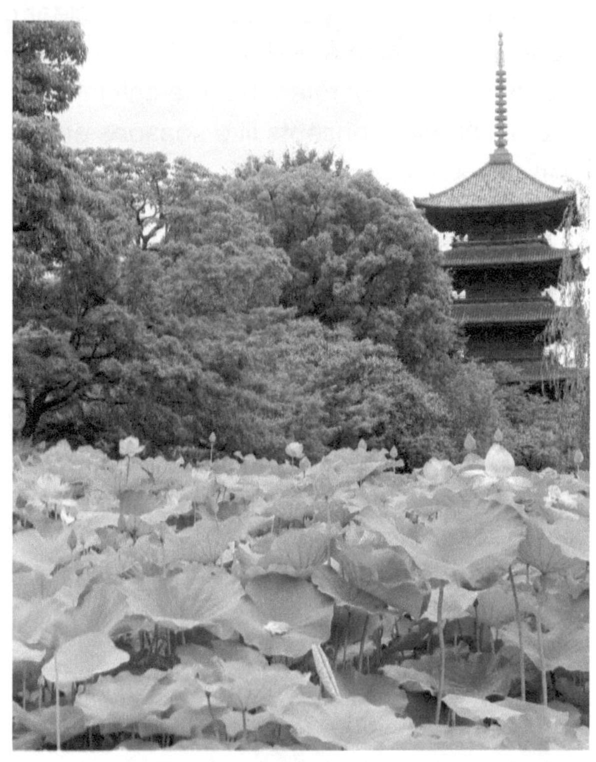

To-ji Temple Lotus Pond
東寺蓮花池
Kyoto Japan
Photographed by KS Vincent Poon
2018

Longya Judun
A Zen Poem I

龍牙居遁
禪詩之一

Calligraphy

Calligrapher (書者): KS Vincent Poon (潘君尚)

Content (內容): A Zen poem by Longya Judun (龍牙居遁禪詩一首)

Style (字體): Cursive Script (草書)

Caption (款識): 唐龍牙居遁禪師詩偈壬寅潘君尚一揮 (A hymnal poem by Zen master Longya Judun, year of the Renyin, Kwan Sheung Vincent Poon scribed flowingly with great ease and liberty)

Seal Inscription (鈐印): 君尚 (朱文) (Kwan Sheung Vincent, red characters), 潘氏 (白文) (The Surname of Poon, white characters)

Medium (材料): Ink on Xuan paper (紙墨水本)

Size (尺寸): 58 X 28cm

Year (年份): 2022

朝看花开满树红，暮看花落树还空。
若将花比人间事，花与人间事一同。

唐龙牙居遁禅师诗偈　壬寅法界书一挥

Translation

龍牙居遁 禪詩之一
A Zen Poem by Longya Judun I

1. 朝看花開滿樹紅，
The mornings, I see the flowers bloom, coating the trees with lustrous red,

2. 暮看花落樹還空。
The evenings, I see the flowers fade, leaving the trees bald with nothingness instead.

3. 若將花比人間事，
If one compares flowers with human affairs and reflects,

4. 花與人間事一同。
Flowers and human affairs are one and the same in fact.

(translated by KS Vincent Poon, March 2022)

Remarks

(I)

This Zen-Buddhist (禪宗) poem was composed by Tang Dynasty's renowned monk Longya Judun (龍牙居遁, 835-923 AD) [1,2].

(II)

All tangible things (色相), like flowers, trees, humans, as well as their affairs, are constantly in a state of change. Nothing is ever absolutely changeless, so all things over time are not of concrete existence. Thus, the *Heart Sutra* (《般若波羅蜜多心經》) states, "Form does not differ from Nothingness, and Nothingness does not differ from Form; Form is Nothingness, and Nothingness is Form (色不異空, 空不異色; 色即是空, 空即是色)."[3]

Footnotes

(1).《全唐詩補編》compiled by 陳尚君. Beijing: 中華書局, 1992, p.1475.

(2). 《禪門諸祖師偈頌》compiled by 子昇 and 如祐, Vol.1. Taipei: Chinese Buddhist Electronic Text Association (中華電子佛典協會, CBETA).

(3). KS Vincent Poon, *Calligraphy Meets Philosophy - Talk 1*. Toronto: The SenSeis, 2022, pp.10,14-15.

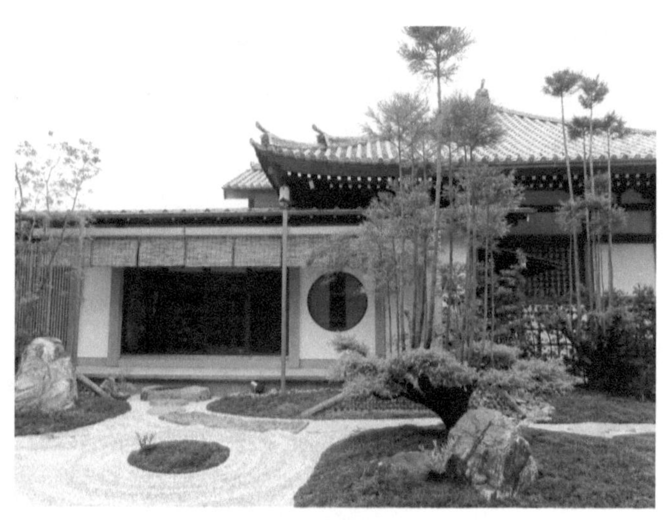

Hasedera Temple Study House
長谷寺書院
Kamakura Japan
Photographed by KS Vincent Poon
2015

Longya Judun
A Zen Poem Ⅱ

龍牙居遁
禪詩之二

Calligraphy

Calligrapher (書者): KS Vincent Poon (潘君尚)

Content (內容): A Zen poem by Longya Judun (龍牙居遁禪詩一首)

Style (字體): Cursive Script (草書)

Caption (款識): 龍牙居遁詩偈壬寅潘君尚一揮 (A hymnal poem by Longya Judun, year of the Renyin, Kwan Sheung Vincent Poon scribed flowingly with great ease and liberty)

Seal Inscription (鈐印): 君尚 (朱文) (Kwan Sheung Vincent, red characters), 潘氏 (白文) (The Surname of Poon, white characters)

Medium (材料): Ink on Xuan paper (紙墨水本)

Size (尺寸): 58 X 28cm

Year (年份): 2022

好心隨處高二不光
去沐事鴉栖未了祇言
如來祕覺法方去不發莊

龍牙居遁詩偈壬寅沖光昌一揮

Translation

龍牙居遁 禪詩之二
A Zen poem by Longya Judun II

1. 將心除妄妄難忘，
Taking one's mind off delusions makes delusions hard to forget,

2. 不體玄微事轉忙。
Not living by (體)[1] the Most Profound and Wonderful Way (玄微)[2] makes all kinds of things onerous (忙) instead (轉)[3].

3. 未了衹言如來秘，
Without understanding (了)[4], one always says Tathâgata (如來) is mysterious,

4. 覺後方知不覆藏。
Upon enlightenment, one shall know it was never inconspicuous.

(translated by KS Vincent Poon, September 2022)

Remarks

This Zen-Buddhist (禪宗) poem was composed by monk Longya Judun (龍牙居遁, 835-923 AD) during the Tang Dynasty[5,6].

Footnotes

(1). "體" here means "living by (依照)", as in *Guanzi - Jun Chen I* (《管子•君臣上》): "衣服緤綩, 盡有法度, 則君體法而立." 尹知章 annotated: "體, 猶依也." See Taiwan's 中央研究院《搜詞尋字》 online edition.

(2). "玄微" here means "a profound and wonderful way (深遠微妙的義理)", as in Li Jingliang's (李景亮) *Biography of Li Zhangwu* (《李章武傳》): "以章武精敏, 每訪辨論, 皆洞達玄微, 研究原本, 時人比晉之張華." See 《漢語大詞典》. Shanghai: 上海辭書出版社, 2008, p.2064. "玄微" is thus here translated as the Most Profound and Wonderful Way, which refers to the Way of Buddha (佛理).

(3). "轉" here means "instead (反而/何更)", as in *Book of Poetry - Minor Odes of the Kingdom - Gu Feng* (《詩•小雅•谷風》): "將恐將懼, 維予與女; 將安將樂, 女轉棄予." 孔穎達 annotated: "汝何更棄我乎?" See Taiwan's 中央研究院《搜詞尋字》 online edition.

(4). "了" here means "understanding (明白)", as in *History of the Southern Dynasties - Biography of Tao Hongjing* (《南史•陶弘景傳》): "心如明鏡, 遇物便了." See 李延壽《南史》, Vol.76. Beijing: 中華書局, 1975, p.1898.

(5). 《全唐詩補編》 compiled by 陳尚君. Beijing: 中華書局, 1992, p.1474.

(6). 《禪門諸祖師偈頌》 compiled by 子昇 and 如祐, Vol.1. Taipei: Chinese Buddhist Electronic Text Association (中華電子佛典協會, CBETA).

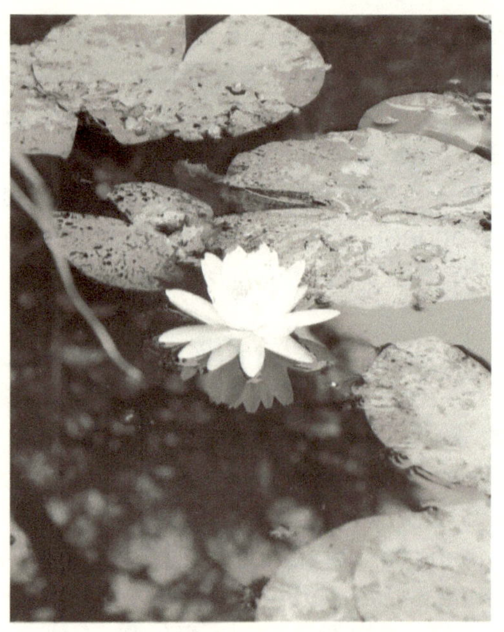

A Water Lily in Kofukuji Temple
興福寺睡蓮
Nagasaki Japan
Photographed by KS Vincent Poon
2023

Longya Judun
A Zen Poem III

龍牙居遁
禪詩之三

Calligraphy

Calligrapher (書者): KS Vincent Poon (潘君尚)

Content (內容): A Zen poem by Longya Judun (龍牙居遁禪詩一首)

Style (字體): Clerical Script (隸書)

Caption (款識): 二千二十三年夏讀龍牙居遁禪師詩句潘君尚 (The year two-thousand twenty-three, summer, reading Zen master Longya Judun's poetic verses, Kwan Sheung Vincent Poon)

Seal Inscription (鈐印): 潘 (朱文) (Poon, red character), 君尚 (白文) (Kwan Sheung Vincent, white characters)

Medium (材料): Ink on Xuan paper (紙墨水本)

Size (尺寸): 95 X 42cm

Year (年份): 2023

三事無憂樂道情且隔雲
水不求名任渠更作千般
解體自無瑕不染青

二十廿三年夏演於丘居選詩四句白沐果尚

Translation

龍牙居遁 禪詩之三
A Zen poem by Longya Judun III

1. 三事無憂樂道情,
Living the Three Deeds (三事)[1], free of worries, I joyfully chant a melody (道情)[2],

2. 且陪雲水不求名。
Only (且)[3] accompanying the clouds and waters, I never seek fame nor glory.

3. 任渠更作千般解,
Let (任) others (渠)[4] nevertheless (更)[5] interpret (解) that in all sorts of ways (千般)[6],

4. 體自無瑕不染青。
My nature (體)[7] inherently can never be blemished (瑕)[8] nor stained gray.

(translated by KS Vincent Poon, September 2022)

Remarks

This Zen-Buddhist (禪宗) poem was composed by monk Longya Judun (龍牙居遁, 835-923 AD) during the Tang Dynasty[9].

Footnotes

(1). In 支謙 《月明菩薩經》:

何等三事? 一者、常護佛深法; 二者、受行佛深法; 三者、諦信佛深法.
What are the Three Deeds? First, the Deed of ever defending
the profound way of Buddha. Second, the Deed of accepting and
practicing the profound way of Buddha. Third, the Deed of believing
concretely in the profound way of Buddha.
(translated by KS Vincent Poon)
Source: 支謙 《月明菩薩經》. Taipei: Chinese Buddhist Electronic
Text Association (中華電子佛典協會, CBETA).

(2). "道情" is a "a type of vocal art that mainly involves singing or
chanting (一種以唱為主的說唱藝術)", as in:

i.《清平山堂話本•張子房慕道記》: "行至半山, 忽見張良漁鼓簡子, 口
唱道情."
ii. 周密 《武林舊事•卷七•乾淳奉親》: "後苑小廝兒三十人, 打息氣唱道
情."
Source: Taiwan's 中華民國教育部 《重編國語辭典修訂本》 online
edition.

(3). "且" here means "only (衹)". See Taiwan's 中央研究院 《搜詞
尋字》 online edition.

(4). "渠" here serves as a pronoun (代詞). See Taiwan's 中央研究
院 《搜詞尋字》 online edition.

(5). "更" here is "nevertheless (縱/雖)". See Taiwan's 中央研究院
《搜詞尋字》 online edition.

(6). "千般"means "all sorts (各式各樣)". See Taiwan's 中華民國教
育部 《重編國語辭典修訂本》 online edition.

(7). "體" here means "nature (本性/本質)". See Taiwan's 中央研究院 《搜詞尋字》 online edition.

(8). "瑕" is often misprinted as "暇", as seen in 《全唐詩補編》 compiled by 陳尚君. The correct character should be "瑕". See 《大日本續藏經•印度支那•第壹輯》 (Japan: Zōkyō Shoin, 1905); as well as 《禪門諸祖師偈頌》 compiled by 子昇 and 如祐, Vol.1 (Taipei: Chinese Buddhist Electronic Text Association, CBETA).

(9). 《禪門諸祖師偈頌》, ibid..

"Withstand and Endure"
with Kuiji's Annotation

"堪忍"
窺基贊文

Calligraphy

Calligrapher (書者): KS Vincent Poon (潘君尚)

Content (內容): Withstand and Endure, with Kuiji's Annotation (堪忍, 窺基贊文)

Style (字體): 堪忍 in Cursive Script (草書), 窺基贊文 in Small Standard Script (小楷)

Caption (款識): 壬寅冬月潘君尚敬書 (A winter month during the year of the Renyin, Kwan Sheung Vincent Poon scribed with due respect)

Seal Inscription (鈐印): 君尚 (朱文) (Kwan Sheung Vincent, red characters), 潘氏 (白文) (The Surname of Poon, white characters)

Medium (材料): Ink on Xuan paper (紙墨水本)

Size (尺寸): 51 X 35cm

Year (年份): 2022

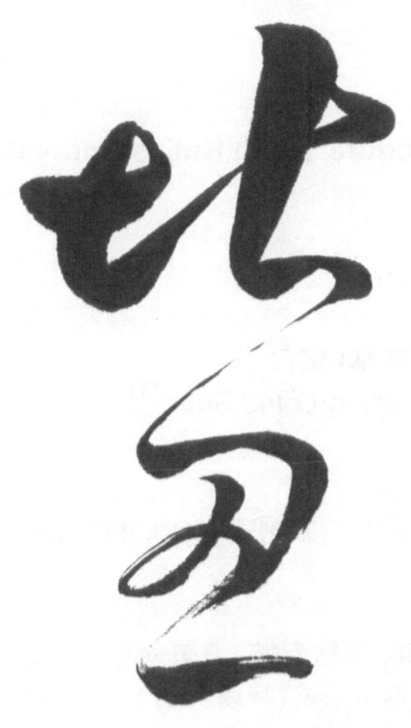

妙法蓮華經贊
曰梵云索訶此
云堪忍諸菩薩
等行利樂時多
諸怨嫉眾苦逼
惱堪耐勞倦而
忍受故因以為
名壬寅冬月潘
君尚敬書

Translation

"堪忍", 窺基贊文
"Withstand and Endure", with Kuiji's Annotation

1. 堪忍。
Withstand and Endure.

2. 《妙法蓮華經》(窺基) 贊曰：
As annotated (by Kuiji) in *Lotus Sutra*[1]:

3. 梵云索訶, 此云堪忍。
In Sanskrit, this is "Saha (索訶)". Here, it is "Withstand and Endure (堪忍)".

4. 諸菩薩等行利樂時, 多諸怨嫉, 眾苦逼惱。
When various Bodhisattvas (菩薩) act to benefit all of the present (樂) and the future (利)[2], they encounter all sorts of discontent (怨嫉), countless (眾) suffering, and aggravating anguish (逼惱) .

5. 堪耐勞倦而忍受故,
Due to (故) them being able to withstand (堪耐) weariness (勞倦) and endure (忍受) it,

6. 因以為名。
a Bodhisattva is hence crowned this title (名)[3].

(translated by KS Vincent Poon, December 2022)

Remarks

"Withstand and Endure (堪忍)" is a term coined by monk Kuiji (窺基, 632-682 AD) of the Tang Dynasty to explain why "The Lord of the Saha World (娑婆世界主)" in the *Lotus Sutra* (《妙法蓮華經》) is "The Lord of the Realm of the Withstanding and Enduring (堪忍界主)".

Footnotes

(1). See Kuiji (窺基) *Annotations of Lotus Sutra* (《妙法蓮華經玄贊》) Vol.2. Taipei: Chinese Buddhist Electronic Text Association (中華電子佛典協會, CBETA).

(2). 《佛學詞典》 . Hong Kong: 菩提學社, publication year unknown, p.254.

(3). This "title" stands for "The Lord of the Saha World (娑婆世界主)" in the *Lotus Sutra* (《妙法蓮華經》). See **Remarks** above.

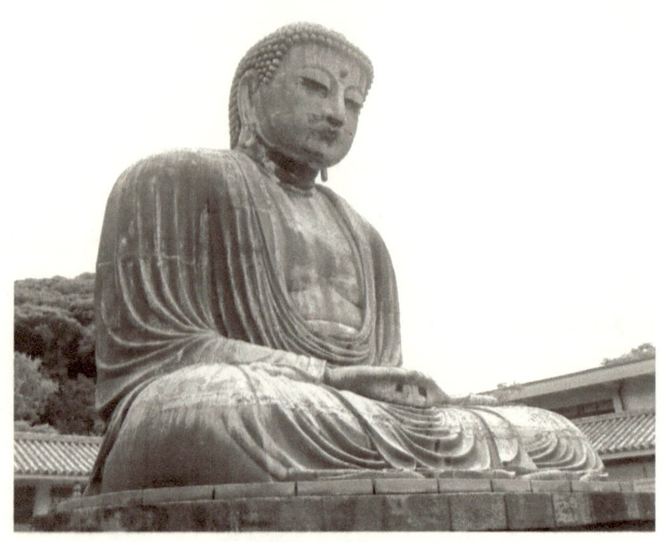

Kamakura Daibutsu
鎌倉大佛
Kamakura Japan
Photographed by KS Vincent Poon
2015

Diamond Sutra

in
Small Standard Script

小楷
《 金剛般若波羅蜜經 》

Calligraphy

Calligrapher (書者): KS Vincent Poon (潘君尚)

Content (內容): *Diamond Sutra* (《金剛般若波羅蜜經》)

Style (字體): Small Standard Script (小楷)

Caption (款識): 金剛般若波羅蜜經潘君尚敬書 (*Diamond Sutra*, Kwan Sheung Vincent Poon scribed with due respect)

Seal Inscription (鈐印): 君尚 (朱文) (Kwan Sheung Vincent, red characters), 潘氏 (白文) (The Surname of Poon, white characters)

Medium (材料): Ink on Xuan paper (紙墨水本)

Size (尺寸): 35 X 137cm each (12 sheets)

Year (年份): 2019

如是我聞一時佛在舍衛國祇樹給孤獨園與大比丘眾千二百五十人俱爾時世尊食時著衣持鉢入舍衛大城乞食於其城中次第乞已還至本處飯食訖收衣鉢洗足已敷座而坐時長老須菩提在大眾中即從座起偏袒右肩右膝著地合掌恭敬而白佛言希有世尊如來善護念諸菩薩善付囑諸菩薩世尊善男子善女人發阿耨多羅三藐三菩提心云何應住云何降伏其心佛言善哉善哉須菩提如汝所說如來善護念諸菩薩善付囑諸菩薩汝今諦聽當

為汝說善男子善女人發阿耨多羅三藐三菩提心應如是住如是降伏其心唯然世尊願樂欲聞佛告須菩提諸菩薩摩訶薩應如是降伏其心所有一切眾生之類若卵生若胎生若濕生若化生若有色若無色若有想若無想若非有想非無想我皆令入無餘涅槃而滅度之如是滅度無量無數無邊眾生實無眾生得滅度者何以故須菩提若菩薩有我相人相眾生相壽者相即非菩薩復次須菩提菩薩於法應無所住行於布施所謂不住色布施不住聲香味觸法布施須菩提菩薩

應如是布施不住於相何以故若菩薩不住相布施其福德不可思量須菩提於意云何東方虛空可思量不不也世尊須菩提南西北方四維上下虛空可思量不不也世尊須菩提菩薩無住相布施福德亦復如是不可思量須菩提菩薩但應如所教住須菩提於意云何可以身相見如來不不也世尊不可以身相得見如來何以故如來所說身相即非身相佛告須菩提凡所有相皆是虛妄若見諸相非相即見如來須菩提白佛言世尊頗有眾生得聞如是言說章句生實信不佛告須菩

佛告須菩提莫作是說如來滅後後
五百歲有持戒修福者於此章句能
生信心以此為實當知是人不於一
佛二佛三四五佛而種善根已於無
量千萬佛所種諸善根聞是章句乃
至一念生淨信者須菩提如來悉知
悉見是諸眾生得如是無量福德何
以故是諸眾生無復我相人相眾生
相壽者相無法相亦無非法相何以
故是諸眾生若心取相則為著我人
眾生壽者若取法相即著我人眾生
壽者何以故若取非法相即著我人
眾生壽者是故不應取法不應取非
法以是義故如來常說汝等比丘知

丘知我說法如筏喻者法尚應捨何況非法須菩提於意云何如來得阿耨多羅三藐三菩提耶如來有所說法耶須菩提言如我解佛所說義無有定法名阿耨多羅三藐三菩提亦無有定法如來可說何以故如來所說法皆不可取不可說非法非非法所以者何一切賢聖皆以無為法而有差別須菩提於意云何若人滿三千大千世界七寶以用布施是人所得福德寧為多不須菩提言甚多世尊何以故是福德即非福德性是故如來說福德多若復有人於此經中受持乃至四句偈等

為他人說其福勝彼何以故須菩提一切諸佛及諸佛阿耨多羅三藐三菩提法皆從此經出須菩提所謂佛法者即非佛法須菩提於意云何須陀洹能作是念我得須陀洹果不須菩提言不也世尊何以故須陀洹名為入流而無所入不入色聲香味觸法是名須陀洹須菩提於意云何斯陀含能作是念我得斯陀含果不須菩提言不也世尊何以故斯陀含名一往來而實無往來是名斯陀含須菩提於意云何阿那含能作是念我得阿那含果不須菩提言不也世尊何以故阿那含名為不來而實無不來是故名阿那含

不也世尊何以故實無有法名阿羅漢世尊若阿羅漢作是念我得阿羅漢道即為著我人眾生壽者世尊佛說我得無諍三昧人中最為第一是第一離欲阿羅漢世尊我不作是念我是離欲阿羅漢世尊我若作是念我得阿羅漢道世尊則不說須菩提是樂阿蘭那行者以須菩提實無所行而名須菩提是樂阿蘭那行佛告須菩提於意云何如來昔在然燈佛所於法有所得不不也世尊如來在然燈佛所於法實無所得

來在然燈佛所於法實無
所得須菩提於意云何菩
薩莊嚴佛土不不也世尊
何以故莊嚴佛土者即非
莊嚴是名莊嚴是故須菩
提諸菩薩摩訶薩應如是
生清淨心不應住色生心
不應住聲香味觸法生心
應無所住而生其心須菩
提譬如有人身如須彌山
王於意云何是身為大不
須菩提言甚大世尊何以
故佛說非身是名大身須
菩提如恒河中所有沙數
如是沙等恒河於意云何
是諸恒河沙寧為多不須
菩提言甚多世尊但諸恒
河尚多無數何況其沙須
菩提我今實言告汝若有

若有善男子善女人以七寶滿爾所恒河沙數三千大千世界以用布施得福多不須菩提言甚多世尊佛告須菩提若善男子善女人於此經中乃至受持四句偈等為他人說而此福德勝前福德復次須菩提隨說是經乃至四句偈等當知此處一切世間天人阿修羅皆應供養如佛塔廟何況有人盡能受持讀誦須菩提當知是人成就最上第一希有之法若是經典所在之處則為有佛若尊重弟子爾時須菩提白佛言世尊當何名此經我等云何奉持佛告須菩提是經名為金剛般若波羅蜜以是名字汝當奉持

蜜以是名字汝當奉持所以者何須菩提佛說般若波羅蜜即非般若波羅蜜是名般若波羅蜜須菩提於意云何如來有所說法不須菩提白佛言世尊如來無所說須菩提於意云何三千大千世界所有微塵是為多不須菩提言甚多世尊須菩提諸微塵如來說非微塵是名微塵如來說世界非世界是名世界須菩提於意云何可以三十二相見如來不不也世尊不可以三十二相得見如來何以故如來說三十二相即是非相是名三十二相須菩提若有善男子善女人以恒河沙等身

命布施若復有人於此經
中乃至受持四句偈等為
他人說其福甚多爾時須
菩提聞說是經深解義趣
涕淚悲泣而白佛言希有
世尊佛說如是甚深經典
我從昔來所得慧眼未曾
得聞如是之經世尊若復
有人得聞是經信心清淨
則生實相當知是人成就
第一希有功德世尊是實
相者則是非相是故如來
說名實相世尊我今得聞
如是經典信解受持不足
為難若當來世後五百歲
其有眾生得聞是經信解
受持是人則為第一希有
何以故此人無我相無人
相無眾生相無壽者相所

何以故此人無我相人相眾生相壽者相所以者何我相即是非相人相眾生相壽者相即是非相何以故離一切諸相則名諸佛佛告須菩提如是如是若復有人得聞是經不驚不怖不畏當知是人甚為希有何以故須菩提如來說第一波羅蜜即非第一波羅蜜是名第一波羅蜜須菩提忍辱波羅蜜如來說非忍辱波羅蜜是名忍辱波羅蜜何以故須菩提如我昔為歌利王割截身體我於爾時無我相無人相無眾生相無壽者相何以故我於往昔節節支解時若有

作忍辱仙人於爾所世無我相無人相無眾生相無壽者相是故須菩提菩薩應離一切相發阿耨多羅三藐三菩提心不應住色生心不應住聲香味觸法生心應生無所住心若心有住則為非住是故佛說菩薩心不應住色布施須菩提菩薩為利益一切眾生故應如是布施如來說一切諸相即是非相又說一切眾生即非眾生須菩提如來是真語者實語者如語者不誑語者不異語者須菩提如來所得法此法無實無虛須菩提若菩薩心住於法而行布施如人入闇則無所見若菩薩心不住法而行布施如人有目日光明照見種種色

人初日分以恒河沙等身布施中日分復以恒河沙等身布施後日分亦以恒河沙等身布施如是無量百千萬億劫以身布施若復有人聞此經典信心不逆其福勝彼何況書寫受持讀誦為人解說須菩提以要言之是經有不可思議不可稱量無邊功德如來為發大乘者說為發

說若有人能受持讀誦廣為人說如來悉知是人悉見是人皆得成就不可量不可稱無有邊不可思議功德如是人等則為荷擔如來阿耨多羅三藐三菩提何以故須菩提若樂小法者著我見人見眾生見壽者見則於此經不能聽受讀誦為人解說須菩提在在處處若有此經一切世間天人阿修羅所應供養當知此處則為是塔皆應恭敬作禮圍繞以諸華香而散其處復次須菩提善男子善女人受持讀誦此經若為人輕賤是人先世罪業應墮惡道以今世人輕賤故先世罪業則為消滅當得阿耨多羅三藐三菩提

則為消滅當得阿耨多羅三藐三菩提須菩提我念過去無量阿僧祇劫於然燈佛前得值八百四千萬億那由他諸佛悉皆供養承事無空過者若復有人於後末世能受持讀誦此經所得功德於我所供養諸佛功德百分不及一千萬億分乃至算數譬喻所不能及須菩提若善男子善女人於後末世有受持讀誦此經所得功德我若具說者或有人聞心則狂亂狐疑不信須菩提當知是經義不可思議果報亦不可思議爾時須菩提白佛言世尊善男子善女人發阿耨多羅三藐三菩提

心云何應住云何降伏其心佛告須菩提善男子善女人發阿耨多羅三藐三菩提心者當生如是心我應滅度一切眾生滅度一切眾生已而無有一眾生實滅度者何以故須菩提若菩薩有我相人相眾生相壽者相即非菩薩所以者何須菩提實無有法發阿耨多羅三藐三菩提心者須菩提於意云何如來於然燈佛所有法得阿耨多羅三藐三菩提不不也世尊如我解佛所說義佛於然燈佛所無有法得阿耨多羅三藐三菩提佛言

如是如是須菩提實無有法如來得阿耨多羅三藐三菩提須菩提若有法如來得阿耨多羅三藐三菩提者然燈佛則不與我授記汝於來世當得作佛號釋迦牟尼以實無有法得阿耨多羅三藐三菩提是故然燈佛與我授記作是言汝於來世當得作佛號釋迦牟尼何以故如來者即諸法如義若有人言如來得阿耨多羅三藐三菩提須菩提實無有法佛得阿耨多羅三藐三菩提須菩提如來所得阿耨多羅三藐三菩提於是中無實無虛是故如來說一切法皆是佛法須菩提所言一切法者即非一切法是故名一切法

身長大須菩提言世尊如來說人身長大則為非大身是名大身須菩提菩薩亦如是若作是言我當滅度無量眾生則不名菩薩何以故須菩提實無有法名為菩薩是故佛說一切法無我無人無眾生無壽者須菩提若菩薩作是言我當莊嚴佛土是不名菩薩何以故如來說莊嚴佛土者即非莊嚴是名莊嚴須菩提若菩薩通達無我法者如來說名真是菩薩須菩提於意云何如來有肉眼不如是世尊如來有肉眼須菩提於意云何如來有天眼不如是世尊如來有天眼

須菩提於意云何如來有慧眼不如是世尊如來有慧眼
須菩提於意云何如來有法眼不如是世尊如來有法眼
須菩提於意云何如來有佛眼不如是世尊如來有佛眼
須菩提於意云何如恒河中所有沙佛說是沙不如是世尊如來說是沙
須菩提於意云何如一恒河中所有沙有如是沙等恒河是諸恒河所有沙數佛世界如是寧為多不甚多世尊
佛告須菩提爾所國土中所有眾生若干種心如來悉知何以故如來說諸心皆為非心是名為心所以者何須菩提過去心不可得現在心不可得未來心不可得

是世尊如來說是沙須菩提於意云何如一恒河中所有沙有如是沙等恒河是諸恒河所有沙數佛世界如是寧為多不甚多世尊佛告須菩提爾所國土中所有眾生若干種心如來悉知何以故如來說諸心皆為非心是名為心所以者何須菩提過去心不可得現在心不可得未來心不可得須菩提於意云何若有人滿三千大千世界七寶以用布施是人以是因緣得福多不如是世尊此人以是因緣得福甚多須菩提若福德有實如來不說得福德多以福德無故如來說得福德多須

如來說具足色身即非具足色身是名具足色身須菩提於意云何如來可以具足諸相見不不也世尊如來不應以具足諸相見何以故如來說諸相具足即非具足是名諸相具足須菩提汝勿謂如來作是念我當有所說法莫作是念何以故若人言如來有所說法即為謗佛不能解我所說故須菩提說法者無法可說是名說法爾時慧命須菩提白佛言世尊頗有眾生於未來世聞說是法生信心不

須菩提彼非眾生非不眾
生何以故須菩提眾生眾
生者如來說非眾生是名
眾生須菩提白佛言世尊
佛得阿耨多羅三藐三菩
提為無所得耶佛言如是
如是須菩提我於阿耨多
羅三藐三菩提乃至無有
少法可得是名阿耨多羅
三藐三菩提復次須菩提
是法平等無有高下是名
阿耨多羅三藐三菩提以
無我無人無眾生無壽者
修一切善法則得阿耨多
羅三藐三菩提須菩提所
言善法者如來說即非善
法是名善法須菩提若三
千大千世界中所有諸須
彌山王如是等七寶聚有

人持用布施若人以此般
若波羅蜜經乃至四句偈
等受持讀誦為他人說於
前福德百分不及一百千
萬億分乃至算數譬喻所
不能及須菩提於意云何
汝等勿謂如來作是念我
當度眾生須菩提莫作是
念何以故實無有眾生如
來度者若有眾生如來度
者如來則有我人眾生壽
者須菩提如來說有我者
則非有我而凡夫之人以
為有我須菩提凡夫者如
來說則非凡夫是名凡夫
須菩提於意云何可以三
十二相觀如來不須菩提
言如是如是以三十二相
觀如來佛言須菩提若以

三十二相觀如來者轉輪聖王則是如來須菩提白佛言世尊如我解佛所說義不應以三十二相觀如來爾時世尊而說偈言若以色見我以音聲求我是人行邪道不能見如來須菩提汝若作是念如來不以具足相故得阿耨多羅三藐三菩提須菩提莫作是念如來不以具足相故得阿耨多羅三藐三菩提須菩提汝若作是念發阿耨多羅三藐三菩提心者說諸法斷滅莫作是念何以故發阿耨多羅三藐三菩提心者於法不說斷滅相須菩提若菩薩以滿恆河沙等世界七寶持用布施

施若復有人知一切法無
我得成於忍此菩薩勝前
菩薩所得功德何以故須
菩提以諸菩薩不受福德
故須菩提白佛言世尊云
何菩薩不受福德須菩提
菩薩所作福德不應貪著
是故說不受福德須菩提
若有人言如來若來若去
若坐若臥是人不解我所
說義何以故如來者無所
從來亦無所去故名如來
須菩提若善男子善女人
以三千大千世界碎為微
塵於意云何是微塵眾寧
為多不須菩提言甚多世
尊何以故若是微塵眾實
有者佛則不說是微塵眾

即非世界是名世界何以故若世界實有者即是一合相如來說一合相即非一合相是名一合相須菩提一合相者即是不可說但凡夫之人貪著其事須菩提若人言佛說我見人見眾生見壽者見須菩提於意云何是人解我所說義不不也世尊是人不解如來所說義何以故世尊說我見人見眾生見壽者見即非我見人見眾生見壽者見是名我見人見眾生見壽者見須菩提發阿耨多羅三藐三菩提心者於一切法應如是知如是見如是信解不生法相

相須菩提所言法相者如來說即非法相是名法相須菩提若有人以滿無量阿僧祇世界七寶持用布施若有善男子善女人發菩提心者持於此經乃至四句偈等受持讀誦為人演說其福勝彼云何為人演說不取於相如如不動何以故一切有為法如夢幻泡影如露亦如電應作如是觀佛說是經已長老須菩提及諸比丘比丘尼優婆塞優婆夷一切世間天人阿修羅聞佛所說皆大歡喜信受奉行

金剛般若波羅蜜經

Remarks

(I)

This work is the full text of the *Diamond Sutra* in traditional Chinese, translated by Kumārajīva (鳩摩羅什,344-413AD)[1]. There are two popular English translations of the *Sutra*: one by William Gemmell from Chinese to English[2] and the other by Max Muller from Sanskrit to English[3].

(II)

The *Diamond Sutra* (Sanskrit: *Vajracchedikā Prajñāpāramitā Sūtra*) is one of the most important sutras (契經) in Buddhist philosophy and is highly regarded in both traditional Chinese and Japanese societies. Originally written in Sanskrit, it has been translated into many languages, including Chinese, Tibetan, Mongol, Mandshu, and English[4]. Its Sanskrit name "Vajracchedikā Prajñāpāramitā" means "Diamond-cutter, the perfection of Wisdom"[5]. It is named as such, for its teachings are believed to be able to cut through all pain and misery like a sharp and hard diamond[6].

(III)

The *Diamond Sutra* outlines many important fundamental Buddhist principles by documenting a discourse between the Siddhartha Gautama Buddha (釋迦牟尼) and his disciple Subhuti (須菩提). This scripture is veritably the essence of Buddhism, for Siddhartha Gautama Buddha once proclaimed:

一切諸佛 ，及諸佛阿耨多羅三藐三菩提法 ，皆從此經出 。

All Buddhas, and all sorts of Supreme Enlightenment Laws, are derived from this scripture. [7] (translated by KS Vincent Poon)

As such, the *Sutra* is an excellent tool for studying the fundamentals of Buddhism, which includes the core principle of "equating all Forms with Nothingness (色空不二)"[8].

(IV)

Renowned German scholar Max Muller (1823-1900), who once translated the *Diamond Sutra* from the original Sanskrit to English, contended that the *Sutra* "is simply the denial of the reality of the phenomenal world" and is an example of "metaphysical Agnosticism" [9]. This sort of conjecture is flawed, for Buddhas never deny the reality of the phenomenal world. Buddhism merely contends all tangible things (Forms, 色) in the phenomenal world are of non-concrete existence (Nothingness, 空), for all Forms are always in a state of Impermanence (無常)[10]. This Impermanence leads all things in the phenomenal world to change and no longer the same in an instant. The *Diamond Sutra* elaborates:

1. 是實相者，則是非相，是故如來說名實相。
The concrete phenomenon is not the phenomenon itself, thus, Tathâgata merely calls it as "the concrete phenomenon".[11]
2. 若見諸相非相，即見如來。
If one sees all sorts of phenomena are not really the phenomena themselves, then one can see Tathâgata.[12]
(translated by KS Vincent Poon)

Footnotes

(1). 窺基,《金剛般若經贊述 》, 《大正新脩大藏經》Book 33. Tokyo: 大藏出版株式會社, 1988, p.125 .

(2). William Gemmell, *THE DIAMOND SUTRA (Chin–Kang–Ching) or PRAJNA–PARAMITA*. London: Kegan Paul, Trench, Trubner & Co., 1912.

(3). Max Muller, *Sacred Books of the East*, Vol. 49, Part II, *The Vajracchedikā*. Oxford: Clarendon Press , 1894, p.109.

(4). Ibid., p.xii.

(5). Ibid..

(6). 勝義叢刊編輯組, 《金剛經白話句解》. Hong Kong: 菩提學社, 1986, p.1。

(7). 窺基, as in footnote (1), p.136.

(8). 《金剛經白話句解》, as in footnote (6), pp.100-102.

(9). Max Muller, as in footnote (3), pp.xiv-xvi.

(10). KS Vincent Poon, *Calligraphy Meets Philosophy - Talk 1*. Toronto: The SenSeis, 2022, pp.14-15.

(11). 窺基, as in footnote (1), p.140.

(12). Ibid., p.133.

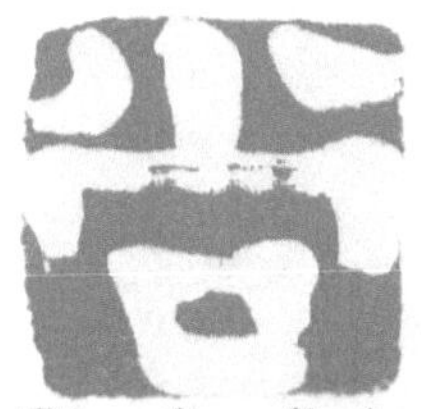

尚尚齋

www.ingramcontent.com/pod-product-compliance
Lightning Source LLC
Chambersburg PA
CBHW022107050726
47591CB00002B/702